Brushstrokes on Water

poems by

Marcia Hurlow

Finishing Line Press
Georgetown, Kentucky

Brushstrokes on Water

Copyright © 2017 by Marcia Hurlow
ISBN 978-1-63534-083-9 First Edition
All rights reserved under International and Pan-American Copyright Conventions.
No part of this book may be reproduced in any manner whatsoever without written
permission from the publisher, except in the case of brief quotations embodied in critical
articles and reviews.

ACKNOWLEDGMENTS

Fishing on Rice Lake, *River Styx*
Fish Story, *Pirene's Fountain*
Three Boys Throwing Pebbles, and Une Pomme de Discorde, *Nimrod*
After Disappointment, *Emrys*
The Sarcophagus of Dihoriaut, *Hermeneutic Chaos*
Country Gamble, *Caveat Lector*
Death Wish of the Phonetician, *2Rivers*
Her Fifth Anniversary Dinner, *The Iconoclast*
Advice for the Vigil, *Red Rock Review*
End of the Season, *Wisconsin Review*
Two Minute Ice Storm, *Pegasus*
Two Landscapes with Windmills, *Sulfur River Literary Review*
The Wife of the Traveling Salesman, *Hawaii Pacific Review*
Maps, *Miramar*
Harmonics, *Southern Poetry Review*
The Etymologist's Revelation, *Avocet*

Publisher: Leah Maines

Editor: Christen Kincaid

Cover Art: Gregory T. Stump

Author Photo: Asbury University

Cover Design: Gregory T. Stump

Printed in the USA on acid-free paper.
Order online: www.finishinglinepress.com
   also available on amazon.com

Author inquiries and mail orders:
Finishing Line Press
P. O. Box 1626
Georgetown, Kentucky 40324
U. S. A.

Table of Contents

Three Boys Throwing Pebbles 1
Fishing on Rice Lake 2
Fish Story 3
Gesture 4
The Tree Surgeon 5
Une Pomme de Discorde 7
The Sarcophagus of Dihoriaut 8
Weigh My Heart, Osiris 9
Country Gamble 10
Death Wish of the Phonetician 11
Canoeing on Our Anniversary 12
After Disappointment 13
Her Fifth Anniversary Dinner 14
End of the Season 15
Advice for the Vigil 16
Two Minute Ice Storm 17
Two Landscapes with Windmills 18
Maps 20
Portrait of Henry Teel 22
Harmonics 23
The Wife of the Traveling Salesman 24
To What Habit Do You Attribute the Longevity of
    Your Marriage 25
Natural History 27
The Entomologist's Revelation 28

With love for
Gregory Thomas Stump
and
Marjorie Hurlow Stump

THREE BOYS THROWING PEBBLES
 —*Karoly Ferenczy, 1890, near Budapest*

Each boy has gathered flat stones
on the sandy bank of the river
to skip clear to the other side,
where we see a clutch of white houses
and a scattering of poplars.

The smallest boy crouches, his back to us.
He reaches down to choose a stone.
The others stand in profile. The oldest,
stone in his right hand, weight
on his right bent leg, may throw soon.

The middle boy, shirtless and barefoot,
stares sternly up the river. We notice
their short-cropped hair glows. Neither
boy smiles. The artist, a man of 28,
knew those were sober faces of loss.

The artist saw the houses were industry,
 the poplars were smoke stacks, the boys
gone off to war, the two not returned.
He picks up the stone and skips it.
It sinks in the middle of the Danube.

FISHING ON RICE LAKE
—Ontario, Canada

So close to night, the waves
are striped, silver and black.

My father, the bubble
in this wooden level,

stands in our fishing boat.
He casts the whistling

gray wand of a pole, writes
on the darkening surface

his one beautiful word.
It conjures a trout then

disappears in the taut line.
When he draws the fish up

it fans the air. Father
dips his hand in the lake,

smoothes down the knife-sharp fins,
edges out the hook, pours

the fish back in the black
water baited with stars.

FISH STORY

There are stories of fish like our stories
of money, subtracting or adding misery.
There are stories of fish like our stories
of God, miraculous and wise, that require
retelling by old women, or men in robes.
When a boy casts out a line and waits
the first time by a river until the pole
genuflects to the current, and with a tug
up flies a golden fish the size of his mother's
fragile hand reaching out from her sick bed
to bless him, which kind of story is this?
Don't answer yet. As his father takes the carp
off the hook, he says it's too small to keep,
hands it to the child to throw back with a kiss.

GESTURE

I stick up my thumb again and call,
"Journeyman, can you give me a ride?"

I have nothing but my promises
and a hobo's bindle of tricks,

but he pulls the reins and stops. He waits,
the question of time in his eyes.

I offer a litany of my trials
and the dim hosannas of my ears.

He opens his ragged gray coat
to reveal a hole in every pocket.

As I climb aboard, he holds up one palm,
then hands me a contract of labors.

I can only raise my thumb, the same
gesture for asking and agreement

THE TREE SURGEON
—*Matthew Hoffman, November 2010, Mt. Vernon, Ohio*

In his car, he watches the river
through soapweed, a small forest
of stems as dense as before their purple
blooms turned to grey, empty pods.

In his basement, the teenage girl,
bound and gagged, awaits the men
who had killed her family beneath
the oak, where he'd watched, raised

and exalted, the silent master
of trees he could mount, saw and shape.
He could predict their growth, follow
their hidden roots: water maple

to the sewer, sugar maple
under sidewalks, the sycamore
tangled in the bedrock broken
by persistence; the swamp beech,

roots straight down as in his school drawings,
though he didn't know the secret
then, what few know, that as it grows
taller, inside it dries, hollows,

a place to hide what he didn't want
back, a place quicker than digging,
more furtive than fire. That's why
the men hired him. He trimmed dead limbs,

bagged the remains, hoisted the four
bodies to the top of the swamp beech
and dropped them down. Soon, he knows, one
of the men, hands bleached clean of blood,

will drop his fee in unmarked bills
through his car window. He hears birds
quiet behind him as the slow
footsteps break the twigs and brittle weeds.

UNE POMME DE DISCORDE
*—French idiom referring to the apple Paris gives Venus,
arousing the hatred of Juno and Minerva*

When I want sweetness, I prepare
to slice it fine, keep the seeds.

I have it. I give it to her.
The equation is simple.

Small and probably red, it poses
on the palm of Venus like a gem.

By giving it to her, I have
not given it to anyone else.

Who holds the apple changes
another with desire and guilt.

Whom do Juno and Minerva hate?
Themselves, for being empty-handed.

She, the egg of love, the dust
of skin, lifts it now and bites.

THE SARCOPHAGUS OF DIHORIAUT
—end of the 22nd Dynasty (ca. 750 B.C.)

The wings across your chest
announce your intentions.
This world, just a passage
full of weapons, sharp, ready
as you are to slide into
the next world. The horse profiled
over your heart wisely looks
away. Beneath him the fish
stays in his world. The sparrow
in the reflective air, shiny
with crystals of earth, gold,
golden sand, blessings of scarab
and morsels of grain, rises
before the horned cattle, the glide
of the southbound snail. These
two bodies at your knees,
bodies with heads of eagles,
attend, abide, await
while striped over the base
of the coffin, the bones
of your feet, your long, painted
toes are losing touch
with the earth you ruled.

WEIGH MY HEART, OSIRIS

I have carried the stones
that honor the pharaoh,
breathed the gold dust
scattered in the sand.

I will not need his heart
scarabs, the amulets
of the heart hieroglyphs
woven into my wrappings.

My heart is full from labor,
tongue taken, eyes blinded.
Welcome me, gentle cow.
Sly jackal, keep me safe.

The bull carries me to the sun
that ended chaos at the start.
Send me with it, down
in the waters tamed by light.

COUNTRY GAMBLE

The spin of the big wheel
starts when walking out the door,
the roulette of rolling off
the bed or staying in a minute
longer than the birds stop singing
about the risk of territory
and radiated worms, acid rain,
the cloud of the next terror
sprayed on the midnight crop.

The little gold ball drops into the slot.
Someone behind the curtain of leaves
calls "black fifty-eight," and a broom
the size of a wire-haired terrier
takes rent and tuition, taxi fare,
change for a twenty, the penny
of the loafer who tarried,
missed the lights, camera, action
of the full moon over the cornfield.

DEATH WISH OF THE PHONETICIAN

Every word kills me.
If there are ghosts
I want to be one
who sits here adrift
in this cushioned
corner of couch
surrounded by back
vowels round as pillows,
who rests to formants
of high front vowels
whistling in time
to tunes of the spheres.
No consonants, please.
Don't obstruct the air.

CANOEING ON OUR ANNIVERSARY

This morning the woods flicker with deer,
the river bank lined with turtles.
Patches of sun angle through evergreens,
tick at the wake of my canoe. Alone
I bend the paddle into silence;
underneath, still disturbances.

That day I had watched for mud
to swirl up like cream to the surface
of coffee. Now bright ripples mirror
the shadows 12 feet down: minnows
swim in long curves like his eyebrows,
his brief smile as I had protested
his plan to dive in for my ring.

Below, grey moss, water-thin, leans back
with the river current. Like me,
it is rooted to a granite
bed of repeated, impenetrable
memory that will not rise up.

AFTER DISAPPOINTMENT

What is missing matters
less this time of night,
everything asleep after
a day's disappointments
save a thin, sieved light
flickering on your stubble
and dark curls. Soon

grackle and finch
will mutter at the moon
that fades with the rhythm
of a train, gone in time
with the slip of false dawn
edging the horizon.

The light disappears.
The dark is steady.
The birds settle back,
wait for the sun, no fear
that the world will lack
what they need, won't be
sufficient one day more.

HER FIFTH ANNIVERSARY DINNER
—"Last Flowers," 1890, Jules Breton

The other flowers in our garden
have browned, rotted under the first snow.
If I hold the thorny stalk far enough,
an arm's length away, the petals of this
rose have an edge of black that hides
its inner decay. In the center
of our table, surrounded by platters
of potatoes, squash and roast, its scent
will brighten the wine and ease his evening
after his slow ride, ever slower ride
back to our home and his not-so-new bride.
In November, the storm clouds screen
the piercing stars and the scythe of the moon.
Perfection, how it fades, is my bouquet.

END OF THE SEASON

In the garden, brown leaves
like scabs of healing
cover where we coaxed up

lettuce and carrots, rolled
over melons and squash
to check for beetles, slugs.

As the fall winds fill
the fence corners and late
weeds sprout on the mulch pile,

we think of how our hands
tilled and planted, tunneled
into the humus to set

and to seed, to cradle
and to root. As the cold comes
we find new tasks for hands,

the strength of fingers,
the pull and press into
the rich darkness of the bed.

ADVICE FOR THE VIGIL

I want to explain the mystery
might be too much, the sudden
beauty blinding and reckless
hands again, again too much.

When the sun rises over unmown
weeds, every heartbeat sprawls
and eats and flies. Cover your eyes,
breathe where stems break through the soil.

Insects from the evening, their high
pitch like tinnitus, go quiet.
Birds claim their space now. Listen
to the calm sleeper close beside you.

TWO MINUTE ICE STORM

Up from the west, hail knifes
through the dusk-dark morning.
Our front porch collects pellets.
The kitchen window dings
like a lid over popcorn.

Still harder, the hail could slice
onto the table, shred
the floor. In would fly grackles
and cowbirds, all bloody
from slamming wall to wall.

Their unbirdlike squeals uncoil
like lightning before they swirl
out the back door on gusts
of rain from a purpled sky,
welcome as sunshine. Leaves

from the water maple, ripped
to the ground, arc back their tips
into grass as if in relief.
We sweep the heavy hail
off the porch. Two thrush dip
their beaks into icy weeds.

TWO LANDSCAPES WITH WINDMILL
—*Friesland, The Netherlands, 1853 and 1932*

The landscape is long grass, a distant windmill.
The cow seems enormous compared to the girl.
White with brown spots, head like an ox's,
it needs to be milked. The girl leans away
with the rope, but only the cow's neck moves
forward, eyes turned to the painter, to us.

The girl sets her mouth, determined, not angry.
The cow's quirks are as routine as the breeze
that has untied her capstrings and pulls at her
blue skirt. The latticed blades of the windmill
must be turning. Everything's in motion
but the cow. The sky is blue except for a grey

brush of cloud to the right. More than a storm
it is metaphor. The war demands conscripts
and we see from her dress she is Mennonite.
Dozens of her denomination have died
for their refusal to fight. In a few days
the girl and her family, nine more families

will board a ship to Britain, then to New York
and a train to Indiana: Nappanee,
Shipshewana, Goshen in 1854
already settled by Amish and Brethren.
After the house and barn are built, her life
will be just the same. She will marry the boy

who gave the cow's tail a brief twist and talked
them all home before the rain. Their three sons
will leave the faith and go to war. Two return
to work the farm; the third becomes a lawyer
and vacations in Holland. Here he stands
in the empty field that was his grandfather's:

The painter makes the man's topcoat twist around
his legs, a shroud, but his hair lifts like a wing.
He watches the windmill on the horizon
turn a slow circle. It is enough. He leaves.

MAPS

Be careful what you love.
My mother loved maps.
She loved tracing the blue
lines, the red lines, looking
up the cities that bloomed
on those stems. She loved
to find their music, recipes
for food whose spices never
existed at her grocery.

She loved Dad's stories
of towns he'd seen in Europe.
Even blighted by war
they were lovely on maps
though she'd never fly
to those gold circles,
ornate as Greek myths.
And as maps of neurons

crossed and disappeared
with age she forgot the map
of her hometown that got her
to her sister's house, brought
her milk and bread. Off that
shrinking grid were storms
and monsters. As we talked

in her yellow kitchen,
the snow gathered like nests
in branches of the maples.
The buzz of a dying
bulb above us, I asked
about her trips to California,
Nevada and a week
in downtown Cleveland.

What a small map to travel
compared to her dreams.
So this is what love does:
reshapes thought, the last
synapses of memory. She
leaned in, confided that on
the way to Paris, she and Dad
had landed in London
just to say they'd been there.

"Portrait of Henry Teel"
   —*Andrew Wyeth, 1945*

A woman once lived here, too. The curtains,
white, eyelet borders, lift in a breeze
at the open window Henry doesn't
look from. Along the buffet, three plates
displayed on their rims are tarnished, tilted.
The oilcloth on the table matches
the dark wine of the fabric underneath.
One chair sits there. Another, its twin,

anchors the second window and Henry
who gazes out to the woods, he the lone
occupant of house and island. Broad boards
of the floor show their grain. Their color
in the shadowed room turns grey. Henry
has a long face, a large nose and eyes
like a sphinx. Lips long closed to speech, his mouth
has faded into his grey complexion.

Outside his window this bright day, in pines
lit against a white sky, there must be birds
writing quick strokes on the horizon,
more animals, some other spirit
that draws him away, not the room that casts
him out. The echoes don't need his witness.
They careen through this sparse space at angles,
her voice on a loop of his synapses.

The mask ghosted at the open door
is not her. Its mouth, agape in drama's
frown, must be Henry's. The face in the grey
brushstrokes on the wall, softer, smaller,
gazes out the same window as Henry,
knows the path through the forest to the pier.

HARMONICS

The lampshade in the living room
rattles on the same frequency
as the six a.m. stop and start
of the garbage truck. I listen

to the plates in the cupboard
shiver at the rinsing of plates
in the dishwasher. You know where
this is leading, why love blooms

in proximity, why anger
one lover brings home from work
causes the other to slam
dinner dishes on the table

for the tenderly prepared meal.
Turn on the music. Hold me still.

THE WIFE OF THE TRAVELING SALESMAN

When you have left again,
this day reduced to a thin
cinder of sunlight caught
on your back fender, the dark
drops faster and repeats
without gathering leaf,
bird or thought, every word
a slight variation not worth
attention, a wavering drone
in the same starless night.

TO WHAT HABIT DO YOU ATTRIBUTE THE LONGEVITY OF YOUR MARRIAGE?

So we're having an argument
about politics—common in our thirty
years of marriage—and our car's off
the road, off the crumbling cliff
and into the cumulus and robin's egg
half a mile before we notice
and only then do we plummet.
The parachute of my pink sunbonnet
slows us—down we rock like that tree-top
cradle until an Acme rocket
shoots a hole like a heart and shatters
our target: a bridge over a mad river
complete with whirlpools to hell (see
those red-tailed devils, pitchforks poised
to pop our tires?) when Daffy Duck
lands on our hood. Despite our warnings
with dingbats aplenty, he dons
a top hat, does a tap dance
(with spats, cane, full orchestration)
which shifts the trajectory
of our Chevy to the six lanes
of mayhem and we try to recall
whose turn it was to pay the car
insurance, the life insurance, and
boing! here we are on a shiny
Acme mattress truck. We have a big
face-sucking kiss so we don't notice
the dark tunnel—oh, suffering
succotash, heavens to murgatroid—
that sloughs us off to a desert
where we hang on matching arms
of a cactus and vultures discuss

the proper spices for such aged
specimens when, as you expected,
the Roadrunner beeps and Coyote's
pinwheel legs spin up enough
turbulence to blow the birds off
screen and us back to this couch,
watching Saturday morning TV.

NATURAL HISTORY

History, marked by treelines,
hawthorns rotting into roofs
of fresh-planed suburbia.

A long, mounded stretch—
once a farm lane, rich
as milk cows driven to pasture.

This sharp rise in the flat field,
much older, a burial
we let no one explore.

Today, as spring reawakens
our small plot of land, I choose,
this once, to plant perennials,

a straight line along the porch,
a circle around the mailbox—
to the future, what roots show.

THE ENTOMOLOGIST'S REVELATION

Tonight in this meadow cleared from forest
the sky glistens, dense with stars, no designs
from mythology, no simple answers
discerned for the countless questions of one
woman. She stands under this cluster

of points, her mind a voodoo effigy
of regrets, desires and her impatience
with sorting the buzz and chirrups of bugs
hidden in the ferns and chicory,
invisible as her path to Thursday.

Now the moon slides above the small leaf
of cloud, and the field turns bright with shadow.
Grasshoppers, crickets and small toads arise
synchronized in a clockwise gesture; gone.

Brushstrokes on Water is Marcia L. Hurlow's sixth collection of poetry. Her first full-length collection, *Anomie*, won the Edges Prize at WordTech. Her poems have appeared in various journals, including *Poetry, Poetry East, Poetry Northwest, Nimrod, Poetry Wales, Stand, Miramar, The Iconoclast, Hawaii Pacific Review, Malahat Review* and *Mudfish*. She is a professor of creative writing, journalism, linguistics and TESL at Asbury University.

www.ingramcontent.com/pod-product-compliance
Lightning Source LLC
LaVergne TN
LVHW041510070426
835507LV00012B/1477